Campbell Leadership Descriptor

PARTICIPANT WORKBOOK

David Campbell

JOSSEY-BASS/PFEIFFER
A Wiley Imprint
www.pfeiffer.com

Center for
Creative Leadership
leadership. learning. life.

Published by Pfeiffer
A Wiley Imprint
989 Market Street, San Francisco, CA 94103-1741   www.pfeiffer.com

ISBN: 978-0-7879-5979-1

Center for
Creative Leadership
leadership. learning. life.

For additional copies of the Campbell Leadership Descriptor call Customer Service at (800) 274-4434.

Pfeiffer books and products are available through most bookstores. To contact Pfeiffer directly call our Customer Care Department within the U.S. at (800) 956-7739, outside the U.S. at (317) 572-3986 or fax (317) 572-4002.

Pfeiffer also publishes its books in a variety of electronic formats. Some content that appears in print may not be available in electronic books.

Acquiring Editor: Matthew Davis   Senior Production Editor: Dawn Kilgore
Director of Development: Kathleen Dolan Davies   Manufacturing Supervisor: Becky Carreño
Developmental Editor: Janis Fisher Chan   Interior Design: Leigh McLellan
Editor: Rebecca Taff   Cover Design: Bruce Lundquist

Printed in the United States of America

Printing 20   19   18   17   16   15   14   13   12

Contents

Introduction

In our increasingly complex world, the need for good leadership has never been greater—leadership that can help educate our children, keep us healthy, create greater economic prosperity, add beauty to our world through the arts, help us push back the curtains of ignorance, and lead to harmonious relationships between different populations all over the world. In fact, effective leadership is crucial to the success of any organization. But what is a "good" leader, and how can you improve your chances of success in leadership roles?

The *Campbell Leadership Descriptor* can help you answer those questions. The Descriptor is a short questionnaire that has been designed to help you think about the essential, universal components of leadership that are applicable in all settings, no matter where you live or work. Whether you are leading a small group, such as a committee or a team, or an entire organization, such as a corporation or a government agency, the process of completing the Descriptor and evaluating the results will help you to identify your leadership strengths, to target specific areas for improvement, and to come up with an action plan for becoming a better leader.

About This Workbook

This Participant Workbook provides the detailed information that you need to complete the *Campbell Leadership Descriptor,* understand the results, and use the results to improve your leadership skills. It includes:

- A detailed description of the Descriptor;
- Instructions for completing and scoring the questionnaire;
- Questions to help you think about and evaluate the results;
- Detailed instructions for using the results to develop a Personal Action Plan;
- Suggestions for continuing to improve your leadership skills;

- Frequently asked questions about the Descriptor; and

- A list of recommended reading to further your understanding of leadership.

Your Leadership Challenges

Before proceeding, use the space below to list some of the leadership challenges that face you and your organization in today's environment.

Learning Objectives

After you have completed this Participant Workbook, you will be able to do the following:

- Describe the major components of leadership;

- Identify the characteristics of a successful leader by comparing a "good" leader with a "poor" leader on each of the major components of leadership;

- Evaluate your leadership strengths and weaknesses by comparing yourself with both a "good" leader and a "poor" leader; and

- Develop an action plan for improving your ability to be a successful leader.

Your Personal Objectives

The major purpose of the *Campbell Leadership Descriptor* is to help you to think about the characteristics necessary for effective leadership and to evaluate your own leadership abilities. Before you complete the Descriptor and evaluate the results, take a moment to think about your personal objectives for this process. List some of them below:

The *Campbell Leadership Descriptor*

THE DESCRIPTOR IS A SELF-SCORING QUESTIONNAIRE containing forty adjectives, each focused on a specific leadership characteristic and grouped into nine major components. When you complete and score the Descriptor, you will use the forty adjectives to compare yourself to both a "good" leader and a "poor" leader you have known. The resulting profile will help you identify your own strengths and weaknesses so you can identify actions you can take to be a more successful leader.

The Nine Components

The first six components cover the *major task*s of organizational leadership that must be present and well-executed within any organization so that the organization, and its membership, do not eventually suffer. Normally, it is the organization's leaders who accomplish these tasks, either directly or through delegation.

The remaining three components represent the more *personal* characteristics necessary for successful leadership. Successful leaders must have or be able to develop these characteristics themselves; they cannot be delegated. Without these personal characteristics, no matter how skilled leaders might be in the other six components, they will have trouble focusing the attention and activities of their organization's members.

Six Major Task Components of Organizational Leadership

1. *Vision*—Establish the general tone and direction of the organization.

2. *Management*—Set specific goals and focus company resources on achieving them.

3. *Empowerment*—Select and develop subordinates who are committed to the organization's goals.

4. *Diplomacy*—Forge coalitions with important internal and external constituencies: peers, superiors, subordinates, potential organizational allies, and other important outside decision makers.

5. *Feedback*—Observe and listen carefully to clients, customers, voters, employees, students, team members (that is, all concerned parties) and then share the resulting information in a manner that those affected can accept as beneficial.

6. *Entrepreneurialism*—Find future opportunities, including increased revenues, expanded markets, or a higher probability of desirable outcomes, such as international peace, a healthier environment, or the creation of beauty, through mechanisms such as new projects, programs, or policies.

Three Personal Components of Organizational Leadership

1. *Personal Style*—By personal example, set an overall organizational tone of competence, optimism, integrity, and inspiration.

2. *Personal Energy*—Live a disciplined, wholesome lifestyle that provides the necessary energy and durability to handle the physical demands of leadership: long hours, stressful decisions, conflict and its resolution, and wearying travel.

3. *Multicultural Awareness*—Be experienced and comfortable working with individuals and managing organizations across different geographic, demographic, and cultural borders.

Origin of the Nine Leadership Components

The nine essential leadership components were derived from thirty years of experience with the Center for Creative Leadership's research and training programs on leadership. The list grew out of innumerable studies, projects, conferences, training sessions, and discussions with practicing leaders, particularly those discussions concerning the "core competencies" of leadership necessary in widely diverse organizations.

Although many organizations feel the need to develop an idiosyncratic list of leadership competencies for their own organization, most of their lists overlap substantially with the nine components provided here. For example, a shipping company may have the following item on its core list:

"Ability to coordinate shipping schedules for multiple vessels with multiple cargoes entering and departing multiple ports."

This action can be more generally covered in the "management" component of the Descriptor by adjectives such as the following:

- *Systematic:* Develops systems and procedures for efficiently organizing people and material resources.

- *Focused:* Sets clear work priorities for self and others.

- *Delegating:* Effectively assigns responsibility and the necessary authority to others.

By using these more generalized statements, leaders across a wide variety of organizations can be compared on the nine core components. Not incidentally, the statements can also be used to describe leaders across a range of functions within the same organization, such as operations, finance, marketing, human resources, and information systems.

The Defining Adjectives

For each of the nine components, we have developed a list of five adjectives to describe the characteristics of leaders who are talented in the accomplishment of that component. The specific adjectives that represent each component also derive from the Center for Creative Leadership's accumulated experience. Established assessment instruments of various kinds, including personality surveys, 360-degree leadership questionnaires, and standardized lists of competencies, were particularly useful in identifying which components were central to leadership skills in various settings, and the adjectives selected represent a compilation from all of these sources.

The five adjectives used for each component expand the coverage "bandwidth" and the reliability of the assessment that component provides. Obviously, several related items can cover a broader spectrum of the topic than can a single item, and answers to several items covering slightly different features of a single component provide a more reliable assessment than any single adjective taken alone.

VISION—Establish the General Tone and Direction of the Organization

Adjectives that describe leaders who are successful as visionaries in today's global economy are

- *Farsighted:* Sees the big picture in developing a vision for the future.

- *Enterprising:* Likes to take on new projects and programs.

- *Persuasive:* Presents new ideas in ways that create "buy-in" from necessary constituencies.

- *Resourceful:* Uses existing resources to create successful new ventures.

- *Has a global view:* Thinks beyond national and cultural boundaries.

MANAGEMENT—Set Specific Goals and Focus Resources on Achieving Them

Adjectives that describe leaders who are successful in focusing resources to achieve their goals are

- *Dedicated:* Determined to succeed; will make personal sacrifices for the vision.

- *Delegating:* Effectively assigns responsibility and the necessary authority to others.

- *Dependable:* Performs as promised; meets established deadlines.

- *Focused:* Sets clear work priorities for self and others.

- *Systematic:* Develops systems and procedures for efficiently organizing people and material resources.

EMPOWERMENT—Select and Develop Subordinates Who Are Committed to the Organization's Goals

Adjectives that describe leaders who are good at empowering their people and helping them in their personal development are

- *Encouraging:* Helps others to achieve more than they thought they were capable of.

- *Mentoring:* Provides challenging assignments and related coaching.

- *Perceptive:* Recognizes talent early and provides growth opportunities.

- *Supportive:* Helps others deal with difficult personal situations.

- *Trusting:* Sees the best in others; is not suspicious of differences.

DIPLOMACY—Forge Coalitions with Important Internal and External Constituencies: Peers, Superiors, Subordinates, Potential Organizational Allies, and Other Important Outside Decision Makers

Adjectives that describe leaders who are politically adroit in achieving their organizational agendas are

- *Diplomatic:* Understands the political nuances of important decisions; readily involves individuals and groups who will be affected.

- *Tactful:* Gains goodwill by not being offensive, even when disagreeing.

- *Trusted:* Is trusted by individuals and groups in conflict to be a fair mediator.

- *Well-connected:* Knows a wide range of people who can help get things done.

- *Culturally sensitive:* Develops teamwork among individuals of different cultures, races, religions, and nations.

FEEDBACK—Observe and Listen Carefully to Clients, Customers, Voters, Employees, Students, Team Members and Then Share the Resulting Information in a Manner that Those Affected Can Accept as Beneficial

Adjectives that describe leaders who are excellent in creating and delivering good feedback to their colleagues and their organizations are

- *A good coach:* Gives constructive feedback in a way that benefits individuals.

- *A good teacher:* Communicates critical information needed by groups to perform well.

- *Candid and honest:* Does not suppress information that might be personally embarrassing.

- *Listens well:* Open and responsive when receiving ideas from others.

- *Numerically astute:* Organizes data in informative ways to show trends in individual and organizational performance.

ENTREPRENEURIALISM—Find Future Opportunities, Including Increased Revenues, Expanded Markets, or a Higher Probability of Desirable Outcomes, such as International Peace, a Healthier Environment, or the Creation of Beauty, Through Mechanisms such as New Projects, Programs, or Policies

Adjectives that describe a leader who is successful in creating new endeavors are

- *Adventuresome:* Is willing to take risks on promising but unproven methods.

- *Creative:* Thinks independently and comes up with many novel ideas.

- *Durable:* Persists in the face of criticism or failure; hard to discourage.

- *Good fund raiser:* Adept at securing funds for new projects.

- *Globally innovative:* Enjoys the challenge of creating new programs and projects that go beyond regional and national boundaries.

Although the wide range of leadership tasks covered by these six major categories must be carried out continuously throughout the organization, the people formally in charge, usually termed "The Leaders," must also have the necessary personal, stylistic characteristics to focus their organization on these broadly distributed tasks. For clarity of analysis, these individual characteristics have been gathered into three personal components.

PERSONAL STYLE—By Personal Example, Set an Overall Organizational Tone of Competence, Optimism, Integrity, and Inspiration

Adjectives that describe a leader with an effective personal style are

- *Credible:* Believable, ethical, trustworthy, has few hidden motives.

- *Experienced:* Skilled in and knowledgeable about the organization's core activities.

- *Visible role model:* Understands the symbolic value of personal visibility in both daily and ceremonial settings.

- *Optimistic:* Sees many positive possibilities; is constantly upbeat.

- *Provides an effective global leadership image* across cultural categories and national borders.

PERSONAL ENERGY—Live a Disciplined, Wholesome Lifestyle that Provides the Necessary Energy and Durability to Handle the Physical Demands of Leadership: Long Hours, Stressful Decisions, Conflict and Its Resolution, Wearying Travel

Adjectives that describe a leader who has the necessary personal energy to grapple successfully with the complex tasks of leadership are

- *Balanced:* Adapts well to conflicting personal and work demands.

- *Energetic:* Active, constantly on the go, radiates energy.

- *Physically fit:* In good health, physically durable, seldom sick, has no troublesome addictions.

- *Publicly impressive:* Presents an appealing, energizing leadership image; a good speaker.

- *Internationally resilient:* Comfortable crossing time zones, eating unfamiliar foods, dealing with new customs, and generally adapting to other cultures.

MULTICULTURAL AWARENESS—Be Experienced and Comfortable Working with Individuals and Managing Organizations Across Different Geographic, Demographic, and Cultural Borders

This component recognizes that, with the increasing cultural diversity found in most contemporary organizations and the concurrent expansion of many organizational activities across international borders, leaders at all levels need to be more knowledgeable and sensitive about cross-cultural concerns.

The Multicultural Awareness component has been created by combining appropriate internationally oriented adjectives from five of the other components. The specific adjectives and their related components are

- *Has a global view:* Thinks beyond national and cultural boundaries (*Vision*).

- *Culturally sensitive:* Develops teamwork among individuals of different cultures, races, religions, and nations (*Diplomacy*).

- *Globally innovative:* Enjoys the challenge of creating new programs and projects that go beyond cultural and national boundaries (*Entrepreneurialism*).

- *Provides an effective global leadership image* across cultural categories and national borders (*Personal Style*).

- *Internationally resilient:* Comfortable crossing time zones, eating unfamiliar foods, dealing with new customs, and generally adapting to other cultures (*Personal Energy*).

Completing and Scoring the Descriptor

FOLLOWING THIS PAGE is a sample of a completed *Campbell Leadership Descriptor.* The sample has been filled in to show you how the completed booklet looks.

Notice that the Descriptor includes three response boxes for each of the forty leadership adjectives, one for "self," one for "good leader," and one for "poor leader." The adjectives are grouped into eight clusters. Six clusters represent the six major components of leadership, and two clusters represent two of the three personal style components. The third personal style component, Multicultural Awareness, is constructed by using one adjective each from five of the other components; thus, each of the scoring scales representing the nine components has five adjectives.

Your Name: _____ *Susan* _____

Today's Date: _____

Using the following scale, **write a number in each box or oval** for each statement for yourself, for a good leader, and for a poor leader.

4 = Definitely Descriptive	3 = Descriptive	2 = Not Descriptive	1 = Definitely Not Descriptive

		Self	Good Ldr	Poor Ldr
Vision	1. *Farsighted:* Sees the big picture in developing a vision for the future	4	4	3
	2. *Enterprising:* Likes to take on new projects and programs	4	4	3
	3. *Persuasive:* Presents new ideas in ways that create "buy-in" from necessary constituencies	4	4	3
	4. *Resourceful:* Uses existing resources to create successful new ventures	4	4	3
	5. *Has a global view:* Thinks beyond national and cultural boundaries	4	4	3 *
	Total	20	20	15
Management	6. *Dedicated:* Determined to succeed; will make personal sacrifices for the vision	4	4	2
	7. *Delegating:* Effectively assigns responsibility and the necessary authority to others	3	3	2
	8. *Dependable:* Performs as promised; meets established deadlines	3	4	1
	9. *Focused:* Sets clear work priorities for self and for others	4	4	2
	10. *Systematic:* Develops systems and procedures for efficiently organizing people and material resources	3	4	3
	Total	17	19	10
Empowerment	11. *Encouraging:* Helps others to achieve more than they thought they were capable of achieving	4	4	2
	12. *Mentoring:* Provides challenging assignments and related coaching	3	4	2
	13. *Perceptive:* Recognizes talent early and provides growth opportunities	4	4	3
	14. *Supportive:* Helps others deal with difficult personal situations	4	4	2
	15. *Trusting:* Sees the best in others; is not suspicious of differences	3	3	2
	Total	18	19	11

		Self	Good Ldr	Poor Ldr

Diplomacy

16. *Diplomatic:* Understands the political nuances of important decisions; readily involves individuals and groups who will be affected — 4 | 4 | 3

17. *Tactful:* Gains good will by not being offensive, even when disagreeing — 3 | 3 | 2

18. *Trusted:* Is trusted by individuals and groups in conflict to be a fair mediator — 3 | 4 | 2

19. *Well-connected:* Knows a wide range of people who can help get things done — 4 | 4 | 4

20. *Culturally sensitive:* Develops teamwork among individuals of different cultures, races, religions, and nations — ③ | ④ | ③*

Total — 17 | 19 | 14

Feedback

21. *A good coach:* Gives constructive feedback in a way that benefits individuals — 4 | 4 | 3

22. *A good teacher:* Communicates critical information needed by groups to perform well — 3 | 4 | 3

23. *Candid and honest:* Does not suppress information that might be personally embarrassing — 3 | 4 | 2

24. *Listens well:* Open and responsive when receiving ideas from others — 4 | 4 | 2

25. *Numerically astute:* Organizes data in informative ways to show trends in individual and organizational performance — 2 | 3 | 4

Total — 16 | 19 | 14

Entrepreneurialism

26. *Adventuresome:* Is willing to take risks on promising but unproven methods — 4 | 3 | 1

27. *Creative:* Thinks independently and comes up with many novel ideas — 4 | 4 | 2

28. *Durable:* Persists in the face of criticism or failure; hard to discourage — 3 | 4 | 2

29. *Good fund raiser:* Adept at securing funds for new projects — 2 | 4 | 3

30. *Globally innovative:* Enjoys the challenge of creating new programs and projects that go beyond cultural and national boundaries — ③ | ③ | ②*

Total — 16 | 18 | 10

		Self	Good Ldr	Poor Ldr

Personal Style

31. *Credible:* Believable, ethical, trustworthy, has few hidden motives — 3 | 3 | 1

32. *Experienced:* Skilled in and knowledgeable about the organization's core activities — 3 | 4 | 2

33. *A visible role model:* Understands the symbolic value of personal visibility in both daily and ceremonial settings — 4 | 4 | 2

34. *Optimistic:* Sees many positive possibilities; is always upbeat — 4 | 4 | 2

35. *Looks at global picture:* Provides an effective global leadership image across cultural categories and national borders — (3) | (3) | (2)*

Total — 17 | 18 | 9

Personal Energy

36. *Balanced:* Adapts well to conflicting personal and work demands — 4 | 3 | 2

37. *Energetic:* Active, constantly on the go, radiates energy — 4 | 4 | 3

38. *Physically fit:* In good health, physically durable, seldom sick, has no troublesome addictions — 4 | 4 | 4

39. *Publicly impressive:* Presents an appealing, energizing leadership image; a good speaker — 4 | 4 | 3

40. *Internationally resilient:* Comfortable crossing times zones, eating unfamiliar foods, dealing with new customs, and generally adapting to other cultures — (4) | (3) | (2)*

Total — 20 | 18 | 14

Scoring

1. For each component, beginning with "Vision," add up your five ratings in the "Self" column, including those in the ovals, and write the result in the "Total" box. Do the same for the "Good Leader" and "Poor Leader" columns.

2. Repeat this process for the remaining components.

*3. To total your "Multicultural Awareness" component, add up the five ratings in the ovals (items 5, 20, 30, 35, and 40) for the Self, Good Leader, and Poor Leader columns and write the results in the designated boxes below.

Multicultural Awareness Total — 17 | 18 | 12

4. Using the results from the Total boxes, plot your scores on the profile sheet (page 6) using the symbols on the bottom of the page

Instructions for Completing and Scoring the Descriptor

1. Using the following rating scale, enter a number for each adjective to indicate how well the adjective describes "self," "good leader," and "poor leader":

4 = Definitely Descriptive	3 = Descriptive	2 = Not Descriptive	1 = Definitely Not Descriptive

2. To find the scores for each component except Multicultural Awareness, add up the numbers in the adjective boxes and enter the result in the Total box for that component. The score in each Total box should fall between 5, the minimum possible score, and 20, the maximum possible score.

3. To score the Multicultural Awareness component, add up the five numbers in the oval boxes under the Self column, the Good Leader column, and the Poor Leader column and place the results in the designated boxes at the bottom of page 5.

4. Transfer the totals to the Profile Sheet on page 6 of the booklet, using the following symbols to plot three numbers for each component:

    Self = □   Good Leader = ○   Poor Leader = ▽

5. Draw connecting lines across all of the components for each of the three profiles, using three different colors of ink. The result is a set of three plotted profiles on the nine leadership components: One profile for "self," one for a "good leader," and one for a "poor leader."

What the Descriptor Scores Mean

The implications of the scores are apparent on the Profile Sheet, according to the bands in which the scores fall.

Score	Band	Implications
17 to 20	VERY HIGH	Individual is *very good* in performing these components
14 to 16	ABOVE AVERAGE	Individual is *good* in performing these components
11 to 13	MID-RANGE	Individual's performance is *in the mid-range,* neither high nor low
8 to 10	BELOW AVERAGE	Individual *needs improvement* in performing these components
5 to 7	VERY LOW	Individual *needs significant improvement* in performing these components

Comparing your profile with those of the good and poor leaders you have described will help you recognize your strengths and focus on improvements in areas in which you rated yourself lower than the "good" leader.

Choosing "Good" and "Poor" Leaders for Comparison

When you complete the *Campbell Leadership Descriptor,* you will be asked to describe yourself, along with a "good" leader and a "poor" leader of your choice on each of the nine components. Take a few moments now to think about leaders you have known. Which of them would you consider "good" leaders? Which would you consider "poor" leaders? Why? What makes one person a good leader and another a poor leader? Fill in the chart on the next page with your answers.

Characteristics of Good Leaders	Characteristics of Poor Leaders

Select one of the good leaders you have known and one of the poor leaders you have known to use for comparison when you complete the *Campbell Leadership Descriptor.* Write their names or initials below.

Good leader I have known: _____

Poor leader I have known: _____

Analyzing the Results

IN THIS SECTION, you will review and analyze the results of the question-naire. In the next section, you will discuss strategies for becoming a better leader.

What You Learned

What was the most important thing you learned as a result of completing the Descriptor?

What surprised you?

On which characteristics did your "good" leader score the highest? The lowest?

On which did your "poor" leader score the highest? The lowest?

What do the scores suggest to you about effective leadership?

Did you score higher or lower than you expected? On which characteristics?

In what ways has completing the Descriptor helped you see leadership differently?

What are some things you think you have to do next to be a more effective leader?

Developmental Strategies and Action Planning

YOU HAVE LEARNED ABOUT THE ESSENTIAL COMPONENTS of leadership and have examined your own leadership strengths and challenges. In this section, you will apply what you learned by developing strategies for becoming a more effective leader. You will also begin to develop your Personal Action Plan.

Review Your Descriptor

First, think about what you have learned about your leadership strengths and the areas in which you could improve your leadership abilities. Take another look at your Profile. Examine how you compare with both the good and the poor leaders on each of the nine components. In the space below, list the three components on which you scored yourself the highest and the three components on which you scored yourself the lowest.

Components on Which I Scored the Highest (My Leadership Strengths)	Components on Which I Scored the Lowest (Areas in Which I Need to Improve)

Descriptor Review Questions

For each of the components that you listed above, consider the following questions. Then list actions you can take further to develop your strengths and to strengthen the areas in which you need to improve. There is space on the next pages to write your answers.

For your strengths, consider these questions:

- Why do you think you are strong on this component? How did you develop this strength?
- In what ways will this strength be useful as you move into positions of increasing responsibility and leadership influence?
- What steps can you take to develop this strength further?
- Are there any negative effects of this strength? If so, what can you do to reduce them?

For the areas in which you scored yourself lower, consider these questions:

- Why do you think this area is troublesome for you?
- In what way is this area impeding your progress?
- How important will this area be as you seek increased leadership opportunities?
- What actions could you take to strengthen this area?

Developmental Strategies

Vision

Management

Empowerment

Diplomacy

Feedback

Entrepreneurialism

Personal Style

Personal Energy

Multicultural Awareness

Developmental Activities

NOW THAT YOU HAVE EXAMINED YOUR STRENGTHS as a leader and identified those areas where you need to improve, the next step is to develop an action plan for becoming a more effective leader. Below are some suggestions for developmental activities to improve your leadership abilities in general, as well as specific activities for each of the nine leadership components.

To Improve Your Overall Leadership Abilities

- [ ] Attend professional and personal development courses to learn more about communications skills, negotiating, creative problem solving, presentation skills, time management, team building, goal setting, project planning, management, diversity, and other topics that are essential to leadership success.

- [ ] Take courses to become more creative and learn to think outside the box, such as classes in acting, singing, improvisation, painting, and other areas of art and performance.

- [ ] Look for opportunities to learn something entirely new—and difficult. For example, study a foreign language or learn to play tennis.

- [ ] Find a mentor, someone whose leadership abilities you respect, who is willing to share what he or she knows about leadership, answer questions, and give feedback on your own performance as a leader.

- [ ] Interview successful leaders, asking about their experiences and methods, what they think it takes to be a good leader, and why they think some leaders succeed and others fail.

- [ ] Observe the leaders in your environment and keep a journal in which you record your observations about what they do that works, as well as what they do that does not work.

☐ Look for opportunities to practice leadership in your work environment and with civic, community, or volunteer organizations.

Vision

☐ Consider where your organization is and where it should be going (or, if it is more appropriate, your portion of the organization). Ask questions such as, "What is the 'big picture' of our future?" "What will it take to get there?" For the best leaders, asking these questions again and again comes close to being an obsession. Constantly imagine a future for your organization that excites and motivates you.

☐ Read other leaders' vision statements and think about the ways in which those vision statements drive organizations. For example, Bill Gates' vision, enshrined on a plaque on the Microsoft campus in Redmond, Washington, reads, "Every time a product ships, it takes us one step closer to the vision: a computer on every desk and in every home."

☐ Write a succinct vision statement that captures your thoughts about your organization's future. Outline specific goals that will be necessary to achieve your vision. Imagine how your vision statement might motivate your subordinates, peers, and other relevant groups.

☐ List the resources and the support that will be needed for your vision to succeed and determine where those resources and that support might be obtained.

☐ Predict what the major barriers to progress might be and how they might be overcome.

☐ Observe what other leaders in your environment are doing to create motivating visions and supporting goals. Note which approaches seem to work and which are problematic.

☐ Remain alert for opportunities, including "lucky breaks," that you might exploit to achieve your vision.

☐ Be alert for events that might impede your progress, such as market changes, cultural shifts, or political realignments, and reevaluate your vision in light of changed situations.

Management

☐ Evaluate the way your organization uses its resources and monitors progress toward its goals. What seems to be working, and what seems to need improvement?

☐ Think of and experiment with changes that might improve the way things are done in your organization.

☐ Identify the operational and administrative problems that cause the most trouble in your organization, and work with others to find ways to resolve them. See problems as opportunities for improvement.

☐ Use books, software, training programs, and personal organizers to improve the way you manage your time and organize yourself. Prioritize your activities and keep a "to do" list.

☐ Develop personal systems to organize information, documents, and files so you can easily find what you need.

☐ Discriminate between what you must do yourself and what you can delegate. Learn techniques for delegating so that the right work is done in the right way.

☐ Look for opportunities to delegate, especially in areas that are not your strengths.

☐ Set specific performance goals for yourself, determine what it will take to achieve them, and determine where you will find the necessary resources, including time.

☐ Meet your deadlines.

☐ Work with your subordinates to set specific performance goals. Determine what it will take for people to achieve goals, including what they need from you, and make certain they have the necessary support and resources.

☐ Establish a system for monitoring progress, giving feedback, and revising goals as needed.

Empowerment

☐ Pay attention to what seems to motivate the people around you, identifying the different things that motivate different individuals: For example, one person might be motivated by an increase in salary, another might be motivated by the opportunity to work flexible hours, and still another might be motivated by increasingly challenging projects.

☐ For each of your subordinates, try to identify the primary motivators and, if possible, provide them.

☐ To the extent that you can, involve subordinates in setting the organization's goals, determining how to achieve them, making decisions, and solving problems. When you must make a decision yourself, ask for subordinates' opinions and ideas, consider them carefully, and explain the reasons behind the decisions you make.

☐ Focus on results, not on process. When giving assignments and delegating responsibilities, describe the results you want and encourage the person to come up with a plan for achieving them. Make certain the person has the necessary resources and support to achieve the results.

☐ Think of several ways in which you can provide subordinates with education, training, opportunities for professional travel, increased responsibility, and other activities that help them learn and grow.

☐ Think of several ways in which you can recognize, encourage, and support people who have special talents. For those who appear to have good leadership potential, offer your help as a mentor.

☐ Recognize when productive subordinates need to move on to other opportunities, and be willing to support their decisions.

☐ Try to understand and support subordinates who are dealing with external pressures, such as family problems or health issues.

☐ Think of several ways in which you can help those around you celebrate their successes.

Diplomacy

☐ Rate your interactions with others on a scale of 1 to 10 to determine how often you are in conflict, with 10 being "very often" and 1 being "hardly ever." If you rate yourself higher than 6, you probably need to improve your diplomacy. Identify the reasons for conflicts: For example, do you usually insist on being right? Do you tend to lose your temper when someone opposes or disagrees with you? Do you see compromise as failure? Make a contract with yourself to control the behavior that leads to unnecessary and unproductive conflict.

☐ Learn to listen actively. When involved in complex situations with differing viewpoints, try to understand and respect what is important to each party and work toward a mutually acceptable resolution.

☐ Respect other people, even when you do not agree with them. Consider other people's feelings. Be tactful. Avoid blaming or embarrassing others.

☐ Think of several ways in which you can develop positive relationships with people at different levels of your organization and in other organizations that may be of help to you months or even years in the future.

☐ Find ways to extend your friendships and professional acquaintances to people who are different from you—different points of view, backgrounds, age, gender, race or ethnicity, nationalities, and religions.

☐ Expand your network of contacts by becoming active in professional organizations, civic and community groups, and other organizations.

Feedback

☐ Evaluate the way information is communicated within your organization. Does everyone have the information needed to function effectively? Do you tend to withhold information that is potentially embarrassing, or which you think people do not need? Make a commitment to share information openly, and encourage others to do the same.

☐ Learn how to organize and present numerical data in a way that helps everyone understand its relevance.

☐ Learn how to give useful feedback that helps people know what they are doing well and what they need to improve. Focus on relevant, observable behavior and results instead of assumptions and personalities. Be specific. Say, "I have noticed that you immediately criticized six of the seven ideas that came up in yesterday's team meeting," instead of "You've got an awfully negative attitude!"

☐ Find opportunities in which to practice giving feedback. For example, volunteer to coach a sports team, teach someone to plant a garden, or direct a play.

☐ Ask for feedback from subordinates and peers on your performance, and listen carefully to what they have to say.

☐ Develop systems for people to give and receive peer feedback in a helpful, nonthreatening way.

Entrepreneurialism

☐ Examine several operational or administrative processes in your organization and ask yourself, "How can we do this more quickly, less expensively, or more effectively?" Continually seek new, innovative, creative ways of doing things.

☐ List the obstacles, such as fear of failure or change, that keep you from coming up with new ideas.

☐ Keep a journal or file with new ideas, yours and others,' that intrigue you, including those that may appear to have no relevance to what you are currently doing.

☐ Notice which of the people around you seem to come up with good ideas, and observe what they do to promote acceptance of their ideas.

☐ Learn and practice techniques for generating new ideas, such as brainstorming and thinking outside of the box.

☐ Practice selling your ideas to others. Be specific about what the idea is intended to achieve, why you think it will work, what its benefits will be, and what it will take to achieve results.

☐ Be willing to experiment and risk failure. Not every new idea works, especially not the first time it is tried.

☐ Persist in the face of failure; don't be easily discouraged. Stay focused on ideas and projects you really believe in. Seek and pay attention to feedback that can help you improve your ideas.

Personal Style

☐ Think through the need for and implications of legal behavior—conforming to the laws of our society; ethical behavior—conforming to the ethical standards of your occupation or profession; and moral behavior—conforming to your own internal standards of right and wrong. Imagine situations in which each type of behavior might apply, and determine what you would need to do to behave appropriately.

☐ Practice explaining your ideas and decisions in a way that helps people understand the reasoning behind them.

- [ ] Increase your competence by continually honing your skills in the core activities of your organization. Ask people who know more than you do about certain activities to help you learn.

- [ ] Take courses, such as global marketing or Web design, that increase your level of skill in tangential activities that may be important to your organization, and perhaps your career, in the future.

- [ ] Learn to be an excellent public speaker. Take a presentation skills course or join Toastmasters. Seek opportunities to make presentations to groups of various sizes, both within and outside of your organization. Include cross-cultural or international settings where you might initially feel uncomfortable.

- [ ] Learn to express positive interpretations of events, and develop your sensitivities to issues that are important to others.

Personal Energy

- [ ] Educate yourself about the components of a healthy diet. Eat sensibly and keep your weight under control.

- [ ] Exercise regularly every day, and get sufficient sleep.

- [ ] Do not smoke or use drugs, and drink alcohol only in moderation.

- [ ] Build a network of people to whom you can talk honestly when under stress.

- [ ] Learn methods of controlling stress, such as meditation or relaxation exercises.

- [ ] Periodically involve yourself in rigorous, challenging activities, such as marathons or Outward Bound adventures.

Multicultural Awareness

- [ ] Seek activities that bring you into contact with individuals from different cultures or from other countries. For example, look for opportunities to interact with exchange students, foreign business people, visiting faculty, or other international guests.

- [ ] Actively seek opportunities to travel, study, attend conferences, and work in other countries.

☐ Study another language, listen to music from other countries, and learn to recognize foreign symbols, such as the flags, national anthems, or well-known landmarks of other countries.

☐ Study the histories of other countries.

☐ Attend religious ceremonies for religions different from your own.

☐ Attend ceremonies or celebrations held in the various ethnic communities that comprise our country.

Developing a Personal Action Plan

To pull together everything you have learned and develop a detailed action plan for becoming a more effective leader, complete the Action Planning Worksheet on the following page. The instructions for completing the worksheet follow:

1. In the first column, "What I Want to Improve," enter the specific skills you would like to improve and the goals you want to accomplish. For example, if you scored relatively low on the Feedback component and on Listens Well in particular, you might enter, "Be a better listener."

2. In the second column, "What I Will Do," list specific action steps you will take to accomplish your objective. For example, to "be a better listener," you might take a communication skills class and consciously practice active listening.

3. In the third column, "What I Need & How I Will Get It," enter the resources you will need and how you will obtain them. For example, to take a communication skills class, you might need to seek permission from your manager.

4. In the fourth column, "My Deadline," enter the month and year by which you will have achieved your objective. For example, you might decide that you could reasonably achieve the objective within four months.

Personal Action Planning Worksheet

What I Want to Improve	What I Need to Do	What I Need & How I Will Get It	My Deadline

Key Learning Points

Think about what you have learned through this process. Before you close this Workbook, list several key learning points—the most important things you learned that will help you be a better leader:

Frequently Asked Questions and Their Answers

Where did these nine leadership components come from? Did someone just think them up?

The leadership components are based on thirty years of research and experience at the Center for Creative Leadership. They were derived from observation of recurring themes that appeared in the assessment data on leaders attending the Center's programs; they were also tested against other analyses from several other sources, such as research projects carried out elsewhere; biographies and autobiographies of leaders; and numerous observations of leaders in their native (organizational) environments.

Do these components apply equally well in all settings? For example, are they equally applicable for corporations, government agencies, military units, educational institutions, hospitals, symphony orchestras, and the wide range of nonprofit organizations?

Yes, they apply equally well. The components were selected to represent "universals" in leadership performance. Some components might be more applicable in some settings than in others, and some components might be more applicable than others at specific times—for example, certain components may be more applicable in times of crisis. Still, over the long run, in most organizations at most times, each component is relevant.

I don't have any contact with foreign organizations or foreign workers; how can I answer the questions on the Multicultural Awareness component?

The Multicultural Awareness component addresses differences from one country to another in dealing with leadership and also different cultures, races, and religions. Almost everyone today works with people who are different from themselves in some important ways. In responding to the items on this component, you should consider cultural differences as well as differences between countries.

Why is each descriptor an adjective?

The items provide a description of leaders. Adjectives are an efficient means of description, especially when combined with a more detailed definition. A definition has been included for each adjective to make certain that each respondent interprets the adjective in the same way.

Why are the adjectives grouped into components? Why are they not just analyzed one by one?

First, grouping similar adjectives provides a broader "bandwidth" of coverage than a single adjective taken alone. Second, the total of the answers to several similar adjectives provides a more stable, more reliable score than that of the adjectives considered one at a time.

Why are some of the response positions shaped like ovals?

As you will see when you calculate your scores, the items with the oval response positions are scored on two different components. The ovals help you with those calculations.

Why isn't [some topic, such as persistence or spirituality] included here?

There are two possible answers to this question. In many cases, the topic is in fact included, although perhaps expressed in a slightly different way. Persistence, for example, appears under the component of Entrepreneurialism as the adjective, "Durable: Persists in the face of criticism; hard to discourage."

If the topic does not appear in any form, it might have been considered for inclusion but was rejected because research and/or experience turned up problems with it. For example, the topic of "spirituality" was rejected for two reasons: People differ widely in their interpretation of the topic, and preliminary tryouts failed to find any consistent differences between "leaders" and "non-leaders" on this topic.

What, precisely, is meant by a "good" leader?

By design, no single, fixed definition of "good" leader is given here. The purpose of the Descriptor is to help you arrive at your own definition of a good leader, and then compare yourself to that definition. There is, however, general agreement among respondents that good leaders are people who are characterized by the leadership components described in the Descriptor.

People with these characteristics are almost invariably associated with, and often are in charge of, organizations that are flourishing.

Similarly, what is meant by a "poor" leader?

Again, no single definition is offered here. There is general agreement that poor leaders are not well-described by the items in the Descriptor, and poor leaders tend to belong to organizations or departments within organizations that have unimpressive records of performance.

Do good leaders score high and poor leaders score low on all of the components?

Definitely not. Virtually *all* good leaders have a few flaws, and all poor leaders have at least a few virtues. One of the benefits of the Descriptor is that it provides a detailed description of each person's flaws and virtues, making the person's leadership performance more understandable. The Descriptor also provides a means of focusing attention on possible developmental activities for improvement, even for good leaders.

What kind of people are chosen as "good" leaders? For example, are men chosen more often than women?

Because we do not ask respondents for demographic data on the people whom they choose for either good or bad leaders, we cannot answer this question. It is likely that the distribution of good and poor leaders mirrors the environment. If more men are in leadership roles in a given environment, they are more likely to be chosen for both good and poor leaders.

For certain classroom projects where there was particular interest in the topic of gender and leadership, the respondents were instructed to pick their good and poor leaders from only one gender. According to the facilitators of those sessions, the results strongly suggested that gender was not an important issue. Good leaders of both genders were positively described by the components of the Descriptor, and the reverse was true for poor leaders of both genders.

Will my own scores change over time?

That depends on you. Your current scores probably show some highs, some mid-range scores, and some lows. You should definitely focus on keeping the high scores high; you don't want any changes there. You may choose to focus on mid-range or low scores in an attempt to improve your performance in those areas; thus, those scores might change.

Would my scores change if I completed the Descriptor again in a few days—when I was in a different mood?

Considerable experience with psychological surveys has shown that, yes, you might change some answers slightly if you repeated the survey within a few days. However, the changes tend to be responses to those items that you were somewhat uncertain about. Items that you feel strongly about, either positively or negatively, do not change much, and your strong opinions are what drive your major score patterns.

Recommended Reading

A House Divided: The Diary of a Chief Executive of the Royal Opera House by Mary Allen, 1998. New York: Simon & Schuster. A one-of-a-kind daily record by a CEO under stress, managing the chaos of the London Royal Opera House during a period of financial turbulence. Insightful, fluent, even eloquent, realistic, funny, sad. Not a happy ending.

Ambition: How We Manage Success and Failure Throughout Our Lives by Gilbert Brim, 1992. New York: Basic Books. An illuminating, remarkably insightful book that can help all of us with "self."

Built to Last: Successful Habits of Visionary Companies by James C. Collins and Jerry I. Porras, 1994. (Paperback, 1997). New York: Harper Business. A fascinating, historical study offering valuable insights about the roots of sustained corporate greatness in eighteen visionary corporations, including 3M, Wal-Mart, Walt Disney, Boeing, Sony, and Hewlett-Packard.

Developing Global Executives: The Lessons of International Experience by Morgan W. McCall III and George Hollenbeck, 2002. Boston: Harvard Business School Press. Shrewd conclusions about global management based on the authors' interviews with 101 "exemplary" global managers.

Direct from Dell: Strategies that Revolutionized an Industry by Michael Dell, 1999. New York: Harper Business. A manifesto for revolutionizing any industry, this book provides insight into CEO Dell's drive for improvement, his business logic, and his learning from his mistakes.

Lead On! A Practical Approach to Leadership by David Oliver, Jr., 1992. San Francisco: Presidio. A look at contemporary leadership from an astute admiral's perspective.

Leadership: Enhancing the Lessons of Experience (4th ed.). R.L. Hughes, R.C. Ginnett, and G.J. Curphy (Eds.). Burr Ridge, IL: Irwin/McGraw-Hill, 2001. A college-level textbook for the general student, introducing the subject of leadership. A broad range of coverage. One reviewer calls it "delightfully written."

Leadership Without Easy Answers by Ronald A. Heifetz, 1994. Cambridge, MA: The Belknap Press. A provocative, challenging, fascinating view of "What is leadership?"

Learned Optimism by Martin E.P. Seligman, 1990. New York: Pocket Books. One of the best "self-help" books ever written. It explains how to face the future in good cheer, based on solid psychological research. Especially relevant for those in leadership positions.

Master and Commander by Patrick O'Brien, 1973. New York: W.W. Norton & Company. The first of a series about leadership in the British Navy in the Napoleonic era. Wonderful stuff!

Military Leadership in Pursuit of Excellence (4th ed.). Robert L. Taylor and William E. Rosenbach (Eds.), 2000. Boulder, CO: Westview Press. Readable articles on the contemporary scene, covering a wide spectrum of experience and opinion, civilian as well as military.

Nothing Like It in the World: The Men Who Built the Transcontinental Railroad 1863–1869 by Stephen E. Ambrose, 2000. New York: Simon & Schuster. A highly readable account of the leadership and management qualities necessary to build what is arguably history's most complicated and impactful (pre-space) construction project.

On Becoming a Leader by Warren Bennis, 1989. Reading, MA: Addison-Wesley. Another eloquent, eclectic overview that has enduring relevance for leadership in all segments of society.

On Leadership by John W. Gardner, 1990. (1993 paperback). New York: The Free Press. The best book on leadership fundamentals. Deserves re-reading every year.

Positive Turbulence: Developing Climates for Creativity, Innovation, and Renewal by Stanley Gryskiewicz, 1999. San Francisco: Jossey-Bass. In this readable, practical book, Gryskiewicz distills the wisdom gained in his twenty-five years of working with the world's most creative organizations. The main lesson: Managers can enable and even direct the seemingly random activity that often precedes creative breakthroughs.

Successful Manager's Handbook: Development Strategies for Today's Managers by Susan H. Gebelein, Lisa A. Stevens, Carol J. Skube, David G. Lee, Brian L. Davis, and Lowell W. Hellervik, 2000. Minneapolis, MN: Personnel Decisions International. A dense, 689-page tome, packed with specific suggestions for dealing with management situations. Encyclopedic in coverage, almost daunting in that it makes the reader realize that there are hundreds of managerial behaviors to be learned.

The CCL Handbook of Leadership Development. Cynthia D. McCauley, Russ S. Moxley, and Ellen Van Velsor (Eds.), 1998. San Francisco: Jossey-Bass. A thorough explanation of the elements of leadership development, detailing the many ways that individuals can enhance their leadership skills, including suggestions about how their organizations can help.

The Complete Inklings: Columns on Leadership and Creativity by David P. Campbell, 1999. Greensboro, NC: Center for Creative Leadership. A joyful journey through life's interesting leadership moments by an internationally known psychologist who is also a delightful writer. (This description from an outside observer, Lt. General Walter Ulmer, U.S. Army, Retired)

The Courageous Follower by Ira Chaleff, 1995. San Francisco: Berrett-Koehler. An exciting addition to the leadership library that brings balance to the leadership equation.

The Haldeman Diaries: Inside the Nixon White House by H.R. Haldeman, 1994. Four years and three months of daily diaries, published posthumously. Keen observations and complete frankness. A record of the inexorable failure of an American president with a flawed character, reported through the eyes of a loyal supporter.

The H-P Way: How Bill Hewlett and I Built Our Company by David Packard, 1995. New York: Harper Business. A simple yet extraordinary story of Packard's life and the founding of an extraordinary company. Inspiring in its candor, for example, "More businesses die from indigestion than starvation."

The Lessons of Experience by Morgan McCall, Jr., et al., 1988. New York: Lexington Books. This product of CCL studies of managers is a seminal work that retains its impact.

Transformational Leadership: Industrial, Military, and Educational Impact by Bernard M. Bass, 1997. New York: Lawrence Erlbaum. An excellent academic and practical review of the kind of leadership that produces high-performing units that can function under stress.

Young Men Under Fire by Norman McClean, 1992. Chicago: University of Chicago Press. This book, rapidly becoming a classic, is part detective story, part western, part tragedy, part elegy, and a wholly eloquent ghost story. A painful report of what happens when well-meaning, highly motivated people of limited leadership experience are confronted with a conflagration far beyond their imagination.

About the Author

DAVID CAMPBELL is the Smith Richardson Senior Fellow at the Center for Creative Leadership, where he has been engaged in research and teaching in the area of leadership for twenty-seven years. He has regular contact in the classroom with a wide range of managers and leaders from corporate, governmental, military, and nonprofit sectors. The Center's Leadership at the Peak course, for which Campbell was a co-designer, was cited in 1999 and again in 2001 by *Business Week* survey respondents and *Bricker's International Directory* as the number one short-term leadership development course for top executives in America. He has conducted leadership training sessions in a wide array of U.S. settings and in Peru, the Philippines, Saudi Arabia, Mexico, Australia, Switzerland, Canada, and the United Kingdom. He has been a visiting research fellow at the University of London and a distinguished visiting professor at the U.S. Air Force Academy. He was awarded an honorary doctorate by the University of Colorado in 1998. In 2001, he received The Distinguished Professional Contributions Award from The Society of Industrial and Organizational Psychology (SIOP).

About the Center for Creative Leadership

Founded in 1970, the Center for Creative Leadership (CCL®) is a nonprofit educational institution whose mission is to advance the understanding, practice and development of leadership for the benefit of society worldwide. Each year, CCL teaches thousands of leaders how to enable groups of people to work together in productive and meaningful ways. Practitioners across the world look to CCL for proven, innovative ideas on assessing leadership attributes and improving leadership effectiveness.

The *Campbell Leadership Descriptor* is an assessment tool created at CCL by experts in the field who believe that self-awareness of one's leadership style is an essential first step in identifying key strengths, targeting areas for improvement, and creating a successful action plan for development. Take advantage of the expertise of a world-renowned leadership resource to improve your leadership skills and those of your organization!

For additional CCL information, please visit on the web at www.ccl.org or call 336 545 2810.